# Young Stars
### of NASCAR

by K. C. Kelley
and Bob Woods

 Reader's
Digest
Children's Books™

Pleasantville, New York • Montréal, Québec • Bath, United Kingdom

Copyright © 2005 NASCAR and Reader's Digest Children's Publishing, Inc.
Published by Reader's Digest Children's Books
Reader's Digest Road, Pleasantville, NY U.S.A. 10570-7000
and Reader's Digest Children's Publishing Limited,
The Ice House, 124-126 Walcot Street, Bath UK BA1 5BG
Reader's Digest Children's Books is a trademark
and Reader's Digest is a registered trademark of
The Reader's Digest Association, Inc.
NASCAR® and the NASCAR® Library Collection
are registered trademarks of the National Association
for Stock Car Auto Racing, Inc. All rights reserved.
Manufactured in China.
10 9 8 7 6 5 4 3 2 1


Manuscript and consulting services provided by
Shoreline Publishing Group LLC.


*Library of Congress Cataloging-in-Publication Data*

Kelley, K. C.
    Young stars of NASCAR / written by K.C. Kelley and Bob Woods.
        p. cm.
    ISBN 13: 978-0-7944-0781-0
    ISBN 10: 0-7944-0781-1
    1.  Stock car drivers—United States—Biography—Juvenile literature. 2. Stock car
racing--United States-- Juvenile literature. 3. NASCAR (Association) I. Woods, Bob. II.
Title.

GV1032.A1K45 2005
796.72'092'2--dc22
[B]

                                                                            2004066414

# Contents

# Introduction:

## The Young Guns of NASCAR

The arrival of the millennium in 2000 saw the beginning of a changing of the guard in NASCAR. In the first years of the 21st century, a group of long-time NASCAR heroes moved into retirement. Taking their place was a crew of some of the most talented, exciting, hard-driving youngsters the sport had seen for a long time.

As older drivers move on, team owners look for young talent to take their place. But while today's "senior" drivers came up through the ranks when NASCAR was in a bit of a growing phase, today's drivers come into a sport that ranks among the world's most popular. Today's young drivers have the advantage of millions of dollars of technology, dozens of full-time team members, and nationwide attention for their sport that older drivers didn't always enjoy.

Bill Elliott was a part of NASCAR for more than 25

## Kasey Kahne

## Elliott Sadler

## Jimmie Johnson

## Matt Kenseth

## Kurt Busch

## Ryan Newman

## Tony Stewart

## Dale Earnhardt Jr.

years, racking up 44 NASCAR NEXTEL Cup Series victories and the 1988 championship. However, his last full season was 2004. Rusty Wallace and Terry Labonte are two other former champions putting the checkered flag down on their driving careers in 2005. Even though he finished fourth overall in 2004, Mark Martin will climb out of the driver's seat for the final time in 2005, too.

Hoping to follow in their tire tracks is a pack of young drivers who have earned their rides in a wide variety of ways. The vast NASCAR scouting network watches everything from quarter-mile dirt tracks to asphalt half-miles to dirt tracks in the desert, looking for future stars.

Jimmie Johnson, for example, moved from bouncing trucks through the desert to a pair of second-place finishes in his first three NASCAR NEXTEL Cup Series seasons. It took former open-wheel champ Tony Stewart four seasons to win his first championship. In 2005, former Wisconsin short-course star Kurt Busch matched Stewart's rapid rise.

This infusion of young talent has given NASCAR a big jolt of energy, bringing in new fans and new sponsors. With more and more media attention focused on the sport, having these handsome, chatty, and successful drivers out there in front has helped propel NASCAR to even greater popularity.

All the drivers featured in this book had their first full NASCAR NEXTEL Cup seasons in the 1999 or 2000 seasons or afterward. Several of them were top ten drivers in the initial Chase for the NASCAR NEXTEL Cup in 2004. And all of them expect to make repeat appearances there—and in Victory Lane—in years to come. As you read, you'll see that they have had a wide variety of backgrounds, but all have one goal in mind: Make it to the NASCAR NEXTEL Cup Series…and win it all.

# Chapter 1

## Dale Earnhardt Jr.

A mix of emotions raced through Dale Earnhardt Jr.'s mind as he steered his No. 8 Chevrolet under the checkered flag on July 7, 2001. He had just won the Pepsi 400, barely holding off a late charge by teammate Michael Waltrip during the thrilling final laps of a rare Saturday-night event. It was Junior's first-ever victory at Daytona International Speedway in Daytona Beach, Florida, the sport's most famous track.

Yet as the celebration in Victory Lane began, he couldn't hold off the powerful memory of his father, Dale Earnhardt. Only five months earlier, "The Intimidator" had died after a crash on this very same 2.5-mile oval racetrack.

So on this night, when Earnhardt Jr. zoomed past Johnny Benson in Turn 4 on lap 156—almost the same spot where his father's accident occurred—a spine-tingling feeling surged through the crowd of nearly

Dale Jr.'s shoulder patch sums it up: Young Guns!

150,000 cheering fans. Later at a postrace press conference, Junior addressed a crowd of reporters.

"He was with me tonight," he said of his dad, one of the most beloved, daring, and successful drivers in NASCAR history. "I don't know how I did it. I dedicate this win to him."

Dale Sr. would have been proud of "Little E," one of his son's several nicknames. Junior was following in the family's winning tradition in stock car racing, which dates back to the early, rough-and-tumble years of NASCAR during the 1950s. His grandfather, Ralph Earnhardt, won 250 short-track races and the NASCAR Sportsman Division championship in 1956. At the time, Dale Sr. was a wide-eyed 5-year-old. He would have to wait more than a decade before he first climbed behind the wheel of a race car and launched his legendary NASCAR career.

In the 1980s and '90s, while Dale Sr. was piling up seven NASCAR NEXTEL Cup Series championships, Dale Jr. couldn't help but catch the racing bug, too. Born on October 10, 1974, in Kannapolis, North Carolina—a breeding ground for drivers, including his grandfather and father—Dale Jr. started racing professionally when he was 17. His first race car was a 1978 Chevy Monte Carlo he co-owned with his older half-brother, Kerry Earnhardt. In fact, in those early days he sometimes raced against Kerry and their sister, Kelley.

Junior quickly established himself as the most dedicated and skillful driver in this new generation of Earnhardts. Competing in the Late Model Stock Car division—part of the minor leagues in NASCAR— from 1994-96, he won three times and had an incredible 90 top-10 finishes in 113 starts.

By the end of 1996, Junior had proved himself ready to move up to the series just below the NASCAR NEXTEL Cup. In his first race at Myrtle Beach, South Carolina, he drove a Chevy emblazoned with his grandfather's No. 8, posting a respectable 14th-place finish. He joined the series full time in 1998, winning seven of 31 races, finishing among the top five in 16 races, and earning the series championship.

"I had no idea what to expect or how to run for a

championship," he humbly admitted afterward as he thanked his teammates for their contributions. "So everybody tried to point me in the right direction. We had to learn how to be consistent. Everything was an experience that made me a little bit better person and a little bit better race car driver."

"Little E" dominated the field again in 1999. He took six checkered flags and another title in the series just below the NASCAR NEXTEL Cup Series. He made his NASCAR NEXTEL Cup Series debut that season, too, in the Coca-Cola 600 at Lowe's Motor Speedway in Charlotte, North Carolina. Although he finished 16th among 43 drivers—and couldn't find his pit on his first stop for fuel and fresh tires—he still achieved his ambition to be racing alongside his dad. "He said, 'You did good and stayed out of trouble,'" Junior told reporters when asked about Dale Sr.'s post-race analysis. "I wanted to know he was happy as a car owner and a father."

In 2000, Junior graduated to the NASCAR NEXTEL Cup Series full time. The 25-year-old rookie's first win in the series came in the DirecTV 500 at Texas Motor Speedway in Fort Worth. He dominated the 334-lap event. As he crossed the finish line, nearly six seconds ahead of runner-up Jeff Burton, Dale's teammates heard screams of joy coming from the driver's two-way radio. "I was excited," "Little E" said afterward. "I'm still excited. This is amazing."

Front and center among the well-wishers in Victory Lane stood his biggest fan—Dale Sr., who'd won 75 NASCAR NEXTEL Cup Series races by then and finished seventh that day. "He's something else," the father said after greeting his son with a big hug. "He was talking about coming to Texas and winning his first Cup race. I knew the kid could do it."

Junior came up just shy in the 2000 Raybestos Rookie of the Year voting, 42 points behind winner Matt Kenseth. However, he left no doubt that he was one of the rising stars in NASCAR. He had become the first rookie ever to capture the mid-season All-Star race. In August he made family history, as well, when he lined up against his father and brother Kerry in the Pepsi 400 at Michigan International Speedway. It marked just the second time in NASCAR history that a father and two sons competed in the same event. (The Pettys—Lee and sons Richard and Maurice—did it in 1960.)

Junior would go on to win eight more NASCAR NEXTEL Cup Series races and place among the top 10-finishers 58 times by the end of the 2003 NASCAR season. The first of his two victories in 2003 demonstrated one of the sport's mysteries—how one driver can dominate a particular track. For example, 1960s superstar, David Pearson, won 10 of his 47 races at Darlington Raceway in South Carolina, and Jeff Gordon had five wins in his first 24 starts at Daytona. "Little E" rules at Talladega.

On April 6, 2003, Earnhardt became the first driver ever to win four races in a row at the 2.66-mile superspeedway in Alabama. Incredibly, it marked only his seventh NASCAR NEXTEL Cup Series start at Talladega, although he had won the previous day's minor league event there. His previous finish was eighth place.

This checkered flag at Talladega, however, was checkered with controversy. The Aaron's 499 was an intensely competitive, 188-lap race. There was a 27-car wreck in the opening minutes, 43 lead changes, and a crucial "judgment call" involving Earnhardt. He started at the back of the pack, but kept moving up and eventually took the lead on lap 107. From there, it was a seesaw battle among several drivers to the finish line.

On lap 185, with only Jimmie Johnson and Matt Kenseth ahead of him, Junior passed Kenseth. But his red Chevy came very close to a yellow warning line around the inside of the track. Drivers are not allowed to cross it because it could give them an unfair advantage. Those who do can be penalized. Several drivers claimed that Earnhardt had indeed driven across the line, yet NASCAR officials ruled that he hadn't. "I think it was just one heck of a move more than anything," said Junior. Later that season, Dale Jr. narrowly missed yet another win at Talladega.

And guess what? In 2004 at Talladega, Earnhardt finished second in the first race, and won the other race, too. Both wins were controversial. The Aaron's 499 in April ended unusually under a yellow caution flag following a late crash. Junior's fans protested that he, and not winner Jeff Gordon, was ahead at the time. Then, after his victory in the EA Sports 500 in October, Earnhardt had 25 points taken away for breaking a NASCAR rule for using inappropriate language in a postrace TV interview.

Every point would prove crucial that year. It was the first in which NASCAR held the Chase for the NASCAR NEXTEL Cup, a form of championship playoff spread over the last 10 races of the 36-race season. Only the top 10 drivers with the most points, accumulated in the previous 26 races, would be eligible to challenge for the championship. Junior, enjoying his best season ever, was one of them.

He burst right out of the chute that year, winning the season-opening Daytona 500 in nail-biting fashion. He maneuvered a bold pass of Tony Stewart on lap 180 of the 200-lap race, and then hung tough to the checkers. "In those last laps, I was as nervous as a long-tailed cat under a rocking chair," he joked with the media. "And then finally when you cross the finish line and know you've got the win, it's kind of a relief."

Earnhardt would win five more races in 2004 leading up to the historic season finale Ford 400 at Homestead-Miami Speedway in November. One of five drivers mathematically still in the championship chase behind points leader Kurt Busch, Dale Jr. never could move beyond the pack to take the lead. He finished the race in 23rd place and fell to fifth in the final standings.

"The car was good, but then it went wrong late," he lamented to reporters. "From there on out, it was the worst car I ever drove. It's real frustrating how it gets that way and we can't seem to fix it."

Despite the disappointment, there was certainly nothing wrong with Junior's skills and his

## Dale Earnhardt Jr. Career Statistics

| Year | Starts | Wins | Top-5 Finishes | Total Points | Final Rank |
|------|--------|------|----------------|--------------|------------|
| 1999 | 5 | 0 | 0 | 500 | 48 |
| 2000 | 34 | 2 | 3 | 3,516 | 16 |
| 2001 | 36 | 3 | 9 | 4,460 | 8 |
| 2002 | 36 | 2 | 11 | 4,270 | 11 |
| 2003 | 36 | 2 | 13 | 4,815 | 3 |
| 2004 | 36 | 6 | 16 | 6,368 | 5 |
| Total | 183 | 15 | 52 | | |

determination to get back out there the next season and again chase the championship. Stock car racing is, after all, in his genes.

# NASCAR: It's a Family Affair

The three generations of Earnhardts—Ralph, Dale, and Dale Jr.—represent just one of NASCAR's many famous families. Throughout its colorful history, stock car racing's top series has seen plenty of dads pass their passion for speed down to their children, as well as a bevy of brother acts.

• **The Pettys:** Lee Petty was racing stock cars before NASCAR was formed in 1948. He became one of NASCAR's first superstars, winning the first-ever Daytona 500 and three championships (1954, 1958, and 1959) before retiring in 1964. His son Richard, revered simply as "The King," notched 200 wins and seven NASCAR NEXTEL Cup Series titles in his incredible 35-year career, from 1958-92. He passed the mantle to his son Kyle, now a major figure in today's NASCAR NEXTEL Cup Series.

• **The Labontes:** When Bobby Labonte was crowned NASCAR NEXTEL Cup Series champ in 2000, he joined with his brother Terry to become the only siblings ever to both take the title. Terry debuted in the top series in 1979, and was the points leader in '84 and '96. He had 22 career wins when he announced that

2005 would be his final season. By then, Bobby—eight years his junior—had already taken 21 checkered flags in only 13 years of NASCAR NEXTEL Cup Series competition. Meanwhile, Terry's son Justin is racing in the series just below the NASCAR NEXTEL Cup.

• **The Waltrips:** Today, Darrell Waltrip's fans enjoy his witty commentary as a NASCAR TV analyst for Fox Sports. But from 1972 to 2000, his fans cheered him on through 84 wins, 114 top-10 finishes, and three NASCAR Cup Series championships. On February 18, 2001, Darrell was doing the cheering, though, in the TV broadcast booth as his kid brother Michael—16 years younger—crossed the finish line first in the Daytona 500. Darrell had won NASCAR's most-prestigious event in 1989.

# Chapter 2

## Matt Kenseth

In looking over Matt Kenseth's super-successful racing career, you'll see two words pop up often: patience and consistency. Patience is something he's developed since he was an teenager itching to start his first race. Consistency has been the key ingredient to his many winning seasons. It hasn't always been easy for Kenseth to remain both patient and consistent, but when he does, the results are outstanding.

Consider his phenomenal 2003 NASCAR NEXTEL Cup Series season. Kenseth kept his cool after a disappointing 20th-place finish in the Daytona 500, the first NASCAR NEXTEL Cup Series event of the year. He bounced back and came in third the following Sunday, at Rockingham. Then a week later he won the UAW-DaimlerChrysler 400 at Las Vegas Motor Speedway. That would be Kenseth's lone victory of the season, yet by brilliantly balancing patience with

2003 NASCAR NEXTEL Cup Series champ Matt Kenseth.

consistency, he and his Roush Racing teammates went on to win the NASCAR NEXTEL Cup Series championship.

"There are only 43 of us who get to do this every week," an overjoyed Kenseth said after he locked up the title in the next-to-last race of the season—coincidentally back at the North Carolina Speedway in Rockingham. "It's the top division of stock car racing anywhere in the world, and when you can win races and have everything go right over a 36-race schedule and win a championship, that's a really special thing."

Kenseth's long road to that championship began nearly three decades earlier in Cambridge, Wisconsin, where he was born on March 10, 1972. His dad, Roy, bought a race car when Matt was 13, and that's when the lessons in patience began.

"He made a deal with me," Kenseth remembers. "He would buy the car and race it if I would work on it and keep it up. Then, when I turned 16, I could drive the car. It was hard work, but it was also a great experience and really prepared me to do more than just steer the car."

For three years he learned how to tune an engine, set up the suspension, keep the tires properly inflated, and other necessary preparations for a race. Finally, in

1988 he climbed behind the wheel and competed on some of the most challenging short tracks (paved or dirt racetracks, usually 1/2-mile ovals) in the country.

Just 16 and a junior in high school, he took the checkered flag for the first time in only his third stock car race. At 19, he became the youngest winner ever in an ARTGO Challenge Series race, held in LaCrosse, Wisconsin. In fact, over those three seasons he racked up an incredible 46 victories.

Kenseth slowly but surely worked his way up the stock car racing ladder. He made his debut in the series just below the NASCAR NEXTEL Cup Series on May 25, 1996, in the Red Dog 300 at Charlotte Motor Speedway in Concord, North Carolina. The following year he teamed up with driver-turned-owner Robbie Reiser, who would become an important figure in Kenseth's career. (See the accompanying story.) In 1997, driving Reiser Enterprises' No. 17 Chevrolet Monte Carlo, he ran 21 of 30 Grand National races. He registered two top-five and seven top-10 finishes, giving him enough points to end up second in the battle for the Rookie of the Year award.

Over the next two seasons, Kenseth proved to be a model of consistency. He won a total of seven races, and had 31 top-five finishes and 43 top-10s. He ranked second in the points standings in 1998, third in 1999.

On September 20, 1998, Kenseth saw his longtime dream to race in the NASCAR NEXTEL Cup Series come true when he was called on to fill in for veteran Bill Elliott. Was he ready for prime time when the green flag dropped at the MBNA Gold 400 at Dover

Downs International Speedway in Delaware? You bet! Kenseth impressed the fans with a sixth-place finish. In fact, that proved to be the best debut performance by a driver in the NASCAR NEXTEL Cup Series since Rusty Wallace finished second at Atlanta Motor Speedway on March 3, 1980.

Kenseth competed in five NASCAR NEXTEL Cup Series races in 1999, then moved to the top series full time in 2000. He had signed on with Roush Racing, Reiser joining him as his team's crew chief. Together they enjoyed a breakthrough rookie season. On May 28, they celebrated Kenseth's first NASCAR NEXTEL

Matt Kenseth's yellow and black No. 17 race car has become a familiar sight for NASCAR fans.

Cup Series win, as he beat 42 other drivers in the longest race of the series, the Coca-Cola 600 at Lowe's Motor Speedway.

"I'm pretty surprised, but it feels great to win our first race," said Kenseth. He took the lead on lap 375 of the 399-lap event and didn't look back until the checkered flag dropped. "This is huge to be able to adjust from the beginning of the race to the end of the race and a lot of the changes that go on with this track."

Although he didn't win again that year, Kenseth went on to post a total of four top-fives and 11 top-10s. That gave him enough points to claim the coveted Raybestos Rookie of the Year title, just ahead of Dale Earnhardt Jr.

"To finish ahead of that caliber of talent says a lot about the commitment and talent of this race team," Kenseth remarked.

Even with all that talent, in 2001 Kenseth couldn't avoid the dreaded "sophomore jinx." Following his sensational first year, he only managed four top-fives and nine top-10s in his second NASCAR NEXTEL Cup Series season, leaving him 13th in the championship points standings. The brightest spot was that his No. 17 Ford Taurus team won the Pit Crew Competition, changing four tires and dumping a can of fuel faster than any other team.

Kenseth won five races in 2002—more than any other driver on the NASCAR NEXTEL Cup Series, but the inconsistency bug bit him on too many other Sundays. A year later, however, he kept it all together throughout his championship dream season. He charged to the lead in the points standings after the fourth race, and then stayed there for a record 33 consecutive races. Along the way, he notched 11 top-fives and a series-high 25 top-10s.

"We were competitive in every race, even the ones where we had a problem, such as an engine failure or a wreck," Kenseth said. "This team hardly missed a beat all year, and we deserve to be champions. I owe all of the credit to Robbie and the rest of the guys for giving me great cars, which we turned into consistent contenders each week."

Almost before they'd swept up the confetti strewn along Victory Lane, Kenseth's title stirred up an old debate over the long-standing points system. It centered around the fairness of awarding the championship to a driver who'd only won one race versus an eight-time winner, as Ryan Newman was in 2003. Are consistency and a lot of top-10 finishes worth as much as multiple checkered flags mixed in with so-so finishes?

NASCAR had grappled with that sticky issue for years, then decided to make a dramatic addition in the points system beginning in 2004. The result was the Chase for the NASCAR NEXTEL Cup playoff among 10 drivers over the final 10 events.

Kenseth started the 2004 season in incredibly strong fashion, perhaps looking to prove that his championship was no fluke. After taking ninth place at the Daytona 500, he won back-to-back races, first at his old stomping grounds, Rockingham, then at Las Vegas. Those would be Kenseth's only victories of the year, yet he maintained his typical consistency and ranked fifth among the Chase for the NASCAR NEXTEL Cup finalists after 26 races.

He was the runner-up at the Sylvania 300 in New Hampshire, the Chase opener, but unfortunately went downhill from there. He averaged 21st over the 10 final races. His chance of repeating officially, and literally, went up in smoke when his engine blew in the eighth event.

"I'm not a big believer in luck, but sometimes things just go right and sometimes they go wrong," Kenseth said in summing up the disappointing end to the 2004 season. "This year when things went wrong, we couldn't turn them into something right."

## Matt Kenseth Career Statistics

| Year | Starts | Wins | Top-5 Finishes | Total Points | Final Rank |
|------|--------|------|----------------|--------------|------------|
| 1998 | 1 | 0 | 0 | 150 | 57 |
| 1999 | 5 | 0 | 1 | 434 | 49 |
| 2000 | 34 | 1 | 4 | 3,711 | 14 |
| 2001 | 36 | 0 | 4 | 3,982 | 13 |
| 2002 | 36 | 5 | 11 | 4,432 | 8 |
| 2003 | 36 | 1 | 11 | 5,022 | 1 |
| 2004 | 36 | 2 | 8 | 6,069 | 8 |
| Total | 184 | 9 | 39 | | |

He's proven, though, that being consistent and patient are much more important than being lucky. That's why more than a few NASCAR fans believe that Kenseth can easily turn things around and be a NASCAR NEXTEL Cup champion again.

# Dynamic Duo

No NASCAR NEXTEL Cup Series champion can succeed on his own. Even though there's only one driver, he's not going anywhere without a strong team behind him. And while the driver enjoys the spotlight, the crew chief is the captain of the team. He works behind the scenes to make sure car and driver are in tip-top shape when the green flag drops.

Matt Kenseth and his Roush Racing crew chief, Robbie Reiser, were actually racing rivals in Wisconsin before joining forces in 1997—and they've been a winning combination ever since. At first, Reiser ran his own team, then both he and Kenseth moved to Roush in 2000. Their efforts won Matt the Raybestos Rookie of the Year title that year and the NASCAR NEXTEL Cup Series championship three years later.

"It's great working with him," Kenseth told *Stock Car Racing Magazine* about his crew chief in 2002. "We understand what each other is saying. We don't always agree with what we're saying to each other, but we understand. We have a lot of trust in each other. If I tell him I need something done on the car, need a set-up that I just have to have, I know that I'm going to get it. We have a great relationship on the track and away from the track, too, so it makes it a lot more enjoyable."

## Chapter 3

## Tony Stewart

Tony Stewart didn't join the NASCAR NEXTEL Cup Series until 1999, when he was 29 years old. But in his short stock car career, he has made his mark on and off the track. "Tony the Tiger" has been called lots of names during his spectacular, if somewhat bumpy, NASCAR career. He's been called "hot-tempered," the sport's "bad boy," and a "troublemaker."

The Indiana-born driver has earned his controversial reputation because he's not afraid to mix it up on the track or to speak his mind afterward. On the other hand, that's exactly why the man behind the wheel of the No. 20 Chevrolet is admired by his faithful followers and respected by fellow drivers. The bottom line is whether fans love him or hate him, they also have to call Stewart two other names—"winner" and "champion."

In each one of his first six seasons in the NASCAR

2002 NASCAR NEXTEL Cup Series champ Tony Stewart.

NEXTEL Cup Series, beginning in 1999, Stewart has finished in the top 10 in the championship points standings. When he won the title in a remarkable 2002 campaign, it was Stewart's ninth driving championship since he began racing go-karts at a Westport, Indiana, racetrack in 1978. Over the years, he's won three karting championships, four United States Auto Club (USAC) titles, and one Indy Racing League crown.

Stewart's 2004 NASCAR NEXTEL Cup season—in which he posted two wins, 10 top-five finishes, and 19 top-10s to end up sixth in points—provided a perfect example of the hot-and-cold emotions that surround him. He started the season strong, coming in second in the Daytona 500 after leading the most laps, but losing out to winner Dale Earnhardt Jr. in the closing minutes.

"I wanted to win," a frustrated Stewart said in his post-race interview. "Trust me, if I could have held Earnhardt off, I would have. But there was no holding that kid back. Sunday was his day."

Stewart's record in the next 14 NASCAR NEXTEL Cup Series races was both good and bad. He had three top-five finishes, six top-10s, and several disappointments in between. There was an "incident" during the Aaron's 499 in April. On lap 83, Stewart drove his Chevy down low to the left side of Kurt

Busch. He bumped Busch's car slightly, just enough to trigger a 10-car crash that snared Rusty Wallace, who later said he wanted to "wring [Stewart's] neck."

Then, at the Dodge/Save Mart 350 in June at Infineon Raceway in Sonoma, California, another controversy arose. Rookie Brian Vickers' No. 25 Chevy was knocked out of the race following contact from Stewart. Afterward, Vickers and Stewart had a confrontation in the garage area. A couple of days later, NASCAR fined Stewart $50,000 and docked him 25 championship points, dropping him to sixth place from fifth.

Two weeks later, there was more trouble, at the Tropicana 400 at Chicagoland Speedway in Joliet, Illinois. Stewart was forced to use a backup car when his primary "ride" had trouble, but he was still running great all day. On a restart following a yellow caution flag (all cars must slow down and stay in place during a caution until the problem is cleared up and the green flag is waved to start the race back up), he bumped into the back end of rookie Kasey Kahne's No. 9 Dodge. Kahne crashed and had to drop out of the race. Stewart went on to win, claiming his 18th career NASCAR NEXTEL Cup Series victory.

NASCAR eventually determined that Stewart hadn't done anything wrong, but he was still criticized for his

Tony Stewart holds off Jeff Gordon and Jimmie Johnson on a straightaway.

hard-driving style. Despite all the controversies, though, Stewart worked hard to block out the negative stuff and remained positively focused on racing.

"You're going to have some fans in your favor, you're going to have some that don't like you, and there will be some on the fence that don't know which way to go," he said a few days after the Kahne uproar. "But when it comes time to get in the car, I don't have three different opinions. I've got one job to do, so I go out and do it."

Stewart's no-nonsense approach to racing is nothing new. He's been developing it since he started racing go-karts when he was seven with the help of his father, Nelson.

"He never let me settle for second," Stewart once said about his dad's influence on his success. "He didn't like it when we ran second, and he knew I didn't like it when we ran second. He pushed me to be better."

Those lessons in determination and perseverance, along with his impressive driving skills, proved to be a winning combination by his eighth birthday. Born on May 20, 1971, in Rushville, Indiana, Stewart earned his first go-kart racing championship in 1980 at the fairgrounds in nearby Columbus. He took home the International Karting Federation Championship in 1983 and the World Karting Association national title in '87.

The teenaged Stewart moved up to higher-horsepower, open-wheel racers, called three-quarter midgets in 1989. Two years later he enjoyed a memorable debut season on the United States Auto Club circuit, earning Rookie of the Year honors. He won the USAC Midget title in 1994, and then in '95 became the first driver ever to capture the USAC Triple Crown with victories in the national Midget, Sprint, and Silver Crown series.

"Any time you win a championship, I don't care what kind of division it's in, it means something because you're racing the best in that field," Stewart stated several years later when asked to compare his USAC and NASCAR titles. "It doesn't matter to me what kind of car it is."

By 1996, Stewart was ready for a new challenge—stock car racing. He raced in a handful of minor-league NASCAR events over the next two years. In 1998, he joined the NASCAR team owned by Joe Gibbs, then the former head coach of the National Football League's Washington Redskins. (Gibbs, who had guided the Redskins to two Super Bowl wins, in 1982 and '87, returned to coach the team in 2004.) Following a 22-race season in the minors, Stewart made the giant leap to the NASCAR NEXTEL Cup Series in 1999.

The results during the first half of his rookie season were mixed. Then he shifted into high gear over the last 18 races. Stewart racked up a string of five consecutive top-10 finishes, then celebrated his first NASCAR NEXTEL Cup Series victory in the Exide Select Batteries 400 at Richmond International Raceway in Virginia. Four top-five finishes followed, including back-to-back wins at Phoenix International Raceway and Homestead-Miami Speedway. Those victories sealed his selection as Raybestos Rookie of the Year. The trio of wins was the most by a rookie in NASCAR's modern era. The icing on his inaugural Cup cake was his fourth-place finish in the points standings.

Stewart's six wins in 2000 were tops among all NASCAR NEXTEL Cup Series drivers. A lackluster first half of the season, however, left him ranked sixth in the final points tally. Still, he appreciated what his team had achieved in the series in just two seasons.

"I never would have dreamed that we could have accomplished what we did this year and last year," he said. "I figured if we could be in the top 25 in points by this time, I would be happy."

He was happy enough winding up second in the 2001 standings—with two checkered flags, highlighted by a dramatic win at Sonoma in his first road-course victory. Stewart was absolutely elated to claim the NASCAR NEXTEL Cup Series title in 2002, especially given his disastrous start in that season's Daytona 500. The No. 20 Pontiac (he switched to Chevrolet in 2003) ran great all week during practices and Saturday's qualifying event. Stewart's ride looked like the car to beat coming into Sunday's Great American Race. Only two laps into the 200-lap event, though, the engine blew up—and so did Stewart's high hopes. "It was the motor," said the dejected driver after finishing last. "I just don't know what happened."

Drawing on the spirit instilled by his dad back in his karting days, Stewart immediately rebounded, with two straight top fives. He followed those with a win at the MBNA America 500 at Atlanta Motor Speedway. At that time he was fifth in the points standings. Four different drivers would hold the points lead before Stewart finally took the top spot after finishing second in the EA Sports 500 at Talladega Superspeedway in October with just six races remaining. He didn't clinch the crown until the season finale at Homestead, winning by a scant 38 points over Mark Martin.

"To start the season off the way that we did, and to have kept our focus to go out and get the most points

## Tony Stewart Career Statistics

| Year | Starts | Wins | Top-5 Finishes | Total Points | Final Rank |
|------|--------|------|----------------|--------------|------------|
| 1999 | 34 | 3 | 12 | 4,774 | 4 |
| 2000 | 34 | 6 | 12 | 4,570 | 6 |
| 2001 | 36 | 3 | 15 | 4,763 | 2 |
| 2002 | 36 | 3 | 15 | 4,800 | 1 |
| 2003 | 36 | 2 | 12 | 4,549 | 7 |
| 2004 | 36 | 2 | 10 | 6,326 | 6 |
| Total | 212 | 19 | 76 | | |

week in and week out, I still have a tough time believing what we've accomplished," he said in recapping his roller-coaster championship season. "We didn't do anything magical. We didn't do anything special."

Even his detractors dispute that last point. Like him or not, you have to admire the way Tony Stewart was able to take the bad with the good and end up a winner and a champion.

# Keeping Track of Tony

It's not exactly a "Where's Waldo?" game, but knowing where Tony Stewart is racing some weekends can be quite a challenge. While he followed a path common among many NASCAR drivers—from go-karts to midgets to sprints to stock cars—Stewart has also taken a few detours over his phenomenal career.

Consider his whereabouts on May 30, 1999. He was in the midst of his Raybestos Rookie of the Year season in the NASCAR NEXTEL Cup Series, but he simply couldn't shake his love of open-wheel racing. The same year Stewart joined the NASCAR ranks in 1996, he also debuted on the Indy Racing League (IRL) circuit. Indeed, he won the top rookie honors there, too.

So when Memorial Day rolled around in '99, Stewart pulled off a historic "Double Duty" racing feat in both the IRL's Indianapolis 500 and NASCAR's Coca-Cola 600 in Charlotte, North Carolina. He became the first driver ever to complete both events in the same day. He finished ninth at Indy before jetting off to the night race in Charlotte, where he came in fourth.

Even though Stewart won the IRL championship

the following year, he ranks his 2002 NASCAR
NEXTEL Cup Series title first. "If I had to retype my
resumé tomorrow, I'd put that championship at No. 1,"
he said reflecting on the '02 season. "All of the
championships I've been a part of were hard to
acquire. They had their unique set of circumstances,
obstacles, and challenges to overcome. But my heart
tells me that the championship is my greatest
accomplishment in racing."

# Chapter 4

## Ryan Newman

Most kids are lucky if they're able to ride a bike by the time they're four-and-a-half years old. Ryan Newman was driving race cars at that young age! And he hasn't slowed down since then.

By the time he celebrated his 27th birthday, on December 8, 2004, the pint-size daredevil from South Bend, Indiana, had grown up to become one of the hottest drivers in the NASCAR NEXTEL Cup Series. At the time, he'd just wrapped up his third full season in stock car racing's premiere series, and already had 11 career wins, 44 top-five finishes, and 60 top-10s—all in just 116 races!

The driver of the No. 12 Dodge appeared headed for a 12th victory, in 2004's season-ending heart-stopper of a race at Homestead-Miami Speedway. Then, with just three laps to go, a crash wrecked his day in the Florida sun. "We were so close to earning

Ryan Newman

another win," he said after the frustrating conclusion of the Ford 400, "but it just wasn't meant to be."

Beginning with those preschool days, Newman has grown accustomed to checkered flags. The little kid became a big deal racing quarter midgets, which are souped-up, safer versions of go-karts. He won more than 100 races, a pair of national championships, and eventually induction into the Quarter Midget Hall of Fame.

In 1993, he moved up to larger midget race cars, and continued his winning ways for the next seven years. Newman first climbed into a stock car in 2000, and immediately triumphed in that style of racing, too. On November 5, he made an even greater climb, competing in his first NASCAR NEXTEL Cup Series race, the Checker Auto Parts/Dura Lube 500 at Phoenix International Raceway in Arizona. Although he finished 41st among 43 drivers, the transition to racing's big leagues had gone pretty smoothly.

"It wasn't that difficult," he recalled a year later in *Auto Racing Digest*. "It's more of a learning process. It takes a long time, and I'm not adjusted to it even now. I learn every time I go out on the track."

Newman's education continued on a variety of levels in 2001. He competed in three different stock car series—two ARCA races, 15 races in the series just below the NASCAR NEXTEL Cup Series, and seven NASCAR NEXTEL Cup Series races. He started the year off in typical winning fashion, taking the checkered flag in February at the ARCA Discount Auto Parts 200 at the legendary Daytona International Speedway in Florida. Driving a Ford for the Penske Racing South team, he zoomed into the lead with 12 laps left in the 80-lap race, then held on to capture the victory.

Newman celebrated again in August by winning his first race in the series just below the NASCAR NEXTEL Cup Series—the NAPAonline.com 250 at Michigan International Speedway. "This is a dream come true," he said after leading 119 of 125 laps and keeping future NASCAR NEXTEL Cup Series rival Kevin Harvick in his rearview mirror following a yellow caution flag and restart with 10 laps remaining.

His lessons on the track were earning Newman high marks, but he also was gaining valuable knowledge off the track. He'd graduated with honors from South Bend LaSalle High School in 1996, and while working his way up the racing ladder was taking classes at Purdue University. In August 2001, around the same time he was crossing the finish line first in Michigan, he received a degree in Vehicle Structure Engineering. So besides learning to steer, brake, pass, and other driving skills, he became well versed in the science of speed. (For more on how an engineering degree helps Newman and his teammates, see the story on page 62.)

Team owner Roger Penske, himself a racing legend during the 1970s and 80s on the Indy car circuit (featuring sleek, open-wheel racers like those at the Indianapolis 500), promoted his bright young pupil in 2002. Penske felt confident that Newman was ready to join the NASCAR NEXTEL Cup series full time—and he was right!

Running in the No. 12 Ford, Newman—and his growing legion of fans—enjoyed a spectacular rookie season. He finished in the top 10 in 22 of the year's 36 races, beginning with the season-opening Daytona 500. He started 23rd and came in an impressive 7th. Just competing in The Great American Race was a tremendous thrill for Newman.

Ryan Newman out in front.

Jimmie Johnson's No. 48 Lowe's Chevy has seen more than its share of fast finishes.

Elliott Sadler's pit crew goes to work.

Kasey Kahne, who drives the No. 9 Dodge race car, is one of the up-and-coming stars in NASCAR.

NASCAR fans know who No. 17 is—2003 Champ
Matt Kenseth!

Dale Earnhardt Jr.

Kurt Busch, the 2004 NASCAR NEXTEL Cup Series champion, behind the wheel in his No. 97 Sharpie race car.

Tony Stewart gets ready for another challenging
NASCAR NEXTEL Cup Series race.

In a few moments, these sleek racing machines will be battling for position and a first-place finish.

"I've got huge memories of watching the Daytona 500 when I was young," Newman said later. "It was something to look forward to the entire winter when I was a kid. You would sit down with Mom and Dad and friends and family and watch the race and have fun."

The fun continued throughout that memorable season, during which he notched 14 top-five finishes. He finally won his first NASCAR NEXTEL Cup Series race on September 15, prevailing in the New Hampshire 300 at the 1.058-mile New Hampshire International Speedway in Loudon. Newman started in the number-one pole position for the fourth time that season. He led for 143 laps, and fought off a late charge by two other stars, Kurt Busch and Tony Stewart. Scheduled for 300 laps, the event was shortened because of rain after 207 laps.

"It's awesome," said Newman, who had finished second in the previous two races. "It meant so much, not just to get the checkered flag first, but all the drivers came up and congratulated me. That was awesome. We're competitors, but we're friends, too."

His debut season ended with Newman being named the Raybestos Rookie of the Year. "Our goal was to win races, poles, the rookie title, and finish in the top 10 in points," said the sixth-place finisher in the points championship. "It was a lot, but we did it."

Newman's 2003 Cup season got off to a flying start—literally. On lap 57 of February's Daytona 500, his car got bumped from behind, hard enough to send it into the wall at the top of the track. Moments later, car and driver were airborne, doing several end-over-end barrel rolls on the infield grass before landing. As horrifying as the scene looked, thanks to all the safety equipment inside NASCAR cars, Newman remarkably walked away only a bit sore.

"I was just at the wrong place at the wrong time," he said afterward to an amazed media corps. "That Dodge went for a heck of a ride. I was just hanging on. Disney World doesn't have one of those [rides], I can tell you that."

That seemed to set the tone for what turned into a roller-coaster season of good and bad luck. Even though Newman won the most poles (11), races (8), and top-five finishes (17), and had the second most top-10s (22) of any driver in the NASCAR NEXTEL Cup Series, he only finished sixth in the points standings. That's because of more tough luck in several races, resulting in seven DNFs—the official name for "did not finish." Still, Newman was the runaway winner of the Speed Channel American Driver of the Year Award.

Small wonder, then, that he entered 2004 as one of the preseason favorites to win the NASCAR NEXTEL Cup Series championship. However, it proved to be another up-and-down battle. On the upside, along with a series-best nine poles, he registered two wins, 11 top-five, and 14 top-10 finishes. On the downside, though, crashes, engine and tire problems, and other bad luck left him with nine DNFs.

Nonetheless, Newman was among the top 10 in points after the first 26 races, which qualified him for NASCAR's inaugural Chase for the NASCAR NEXTEL Cup. The last 10 events only brought further frustration—a blown engine in the first race, a win in the second, three straight disappointing finishes, and so on. Finally, with the late crash in the season finale at Homestead, Newman's topsy-turvy season ground to an agonizing halt.

"I always say that I don't really believe in luck and superstition and all that stuff," Newman said in summing up the year. "But, if there is such a thing as

## Ryan Newman Career Statistics

| Year | Starts | Wins | Top-5 Finishes | Total Points | Final Rank |
|------|--------|------|----------------|--------------|------------|
| 2000 | 1 | 0 | 0 | 40 | 71 |
| 2001 | 7 | 0 | 2 | 497 | 49 |
| 2002 | 36 | 1 | 14 | 4,593 | 6 |
| 2003 | 36 | 8 | 17 | 4,711 | 6 |
| 2004 | 36 | 2 | 11 | 6,180 | 7 |
| Total | 116 | 11 | 44 | | |

bad luck, it trailed our team all season. We expected and wanted more."

More poles, wins, and strong finishes are certain to follow a driver as skilled, determined, and successful as Ryan Newman. His recent misfortunes are bound to change, and NASCAR fans will realize how lucky they are to have him around.

# Brains Behind the Brawn

It takes a lot more than tough driving skills to win 11 NASCAR NEXTEL Cup Series races, as Ryan Newman and the rest of his Penske Racing South team did in his first three full seasons in the series. Hundreds of hours are spent designing, building, and setting up any high-tech race car before it ever hits the track. What makes the No. 12 Dodge's crew unusual is the total involvement of the driver every step of the way. Unlike most of his competitors, Newman has a college degree in mechanical engineering.

"My crew chief, Matt Borland, and others on the team also have engineering degrees," says Newman, who enjoys rebuilding vintage cars in his spare time. "So we have a common language and background to work with in trying to make the race car fast. Hopefully that gives us a little advantage."

Newman's education allows him to understand the technology involved in preparing the car's engine, suspension, brakes, tires, and other components before a race. And once the green flag drops, he knows enough to tell Borland if something's not working right.

"The communication between us is really good," says Borland. "You can have a logical conversation with him and he understands the engineering side of it. I can explain to him why we're making a change and he understands it." It all makes for smart racing.

## Chapter 5

## Kurt Busch

Once upon a time, Kurt Busch dreamed of becoming a pharmacist and opening up a chain of drugstores. On November 21, 2004, there were a whole bunch of NASCAR drivers who wished that the 26-year-old Las Vegas native had followed that dream. They wished that he was filling prescriptions somewhere far away that day instead of signing autographs after winning the NASCAR NEXTEL Cup Series championship in Florida.

Actually, Busch was the one who probably wanted something to calm his nerves during the closing minutes of the 2004 season-ending race that won him his first title. "I was sick to my stomach the last few laps," he admitted following the frantic finish of the Ford 400 at Homestead-Miami Speedway. "I had been out there forever. I felt like I had the whole world on my shoulders, and at the same time I felt I was alone."

Kurt Busch has a reason to be smiling—the 2004 NASCAR NEXTEL Cup Series championship.

Busch felt absolutely terrific at the start of the historic race. And why not? The slim, boyish driver of the No. 97 Ford stood all alone atop the points standings as he wrapped up his fourth full season in the NASCAR NEXTEL Cup Series. He was the man to beat among a group of 10 finalists in the inaugural Chase for the NASCAR NEXTEL Cup. Each had accumulated enough points during the first 26 races of the season to qualify for the 10-race playoff to decide the championship. Coming into Homestead, five rivals still had a shot at going home with the gleaming silver trophy. Busch led Jimmie Johnson by 18 points, Jeff Gordon by 21, Dale Earnhardt Jr. by 72, and Mark Martin by 82.

(Here's how the NASCAR points system works: The winner of each race receives 180 points. The runner-up gets 170. From there, the total drops five points for places two through six, four points for places seven through eleven, and three points for finishers in twelfth place or lower. The 43rd, or last-place driver, gets 34 points. Bonus points are also awarded—five for leading at least one lap any time during the race, and an additional five points for leading the most laps. Following the 26th race of the 36-race season, the 10 drivers with the most points, and any others within 400 points of the leader, compete in the Chase for the NASCAR NEXTEL Cup. Those drivers' points totals are adjusted. The first-place driver begins with 5,050 points, the second-place driver with 5,045, third place with 5,040, and so on.)

The NASCAR math meant that Busch didn't have to win the Ford 400 to secure the championship. He only had to finish far enough ahead of his four fellow chasers. While the race had a fairy tale ending, it contained some grim moments, too—which, appropriately enough, pretty much describe the adventurous story behind Busch's entire racing career.

He still had visions of someday wearing a white lab coat when the 14-year-old began competing in so-called dwarf cars (5/8-scale replica models of vintage 1928-48 American-made automobiles) at Parhump Valley Speedway near his home. He and his little brother Kyle—who would also become a NASCAR driver (see the story on page 74)—grew up watching their dad, Tom Busch, race stock cars at local tracks and work on his racers at home.

"My father instilled in me the love for racing," Kurt has said. "That's where it began. There was always a car in the garage, so we were involved very early."

At first, Kurt's racing tales were mostly happy. He

earned the 1994 Nevada State Dwarf Car Rookie of the Year title and the state championship a year later. He advanced to legend cars (5/8 replicas of early NASCAR racers) and excelled in that category, as well, before moving up to stock cars. From 1997-99 Busch won seven races in the NASCAR Featherlite Southwest Series, plus 1998 Raybestos Rookie of the Year honors and the Touring championship in 1999. He accomplished much of this while achieving a 3.6 grade-point average at Durango High School, then commuting home on weekends from the University of Arizona in Tucson.

"It was busy and hard at times," he recalls, "but you do it in order to do what you love doing."

Busch was proving that he did love auto racing— and was quite good at it—and he changed his ambition to becoming a NASCAR NEXTEL Cup Series driver. In 1999, he received an invitation to a talent search sponsored by Roush Racing. Owner Jack Roush, whose teams feature such stars as Mark Martin, Greg Biffle, Matt Kenseth, and Carl Edwards recognized Busch's talent and signed him up to compete in the NASCAR Craftsman Truck Series in 2000. He won four of 24 races, was runner-up to future Roush teammate Greg Biffle for the championship, and was named Raybestos Rookie of the Year.

2004 NASCAR NEXTEL Cup Series champion Kurt Busch puts the pedal to the metal.

That outstanding performance proved enough for Roush to leapfrog Busch, then just 22, over the next NASCAR level and straight into the NASCAR NEXTEL Cup Series. He drove the No. 97 Ford in the final seven races of 2000, then joined the series full time in 2001. And here's when Kurt's previously smooth ride hit some speed bumps. The competition in the NASCAR NEXTEL Cup Series was much more intense. Busch managed a respectable  record of three top-five finishes, six top-10s, and one pole, but also had seven DNFs ("did not finish"), and too many back-of-the-pack results.

"He wasn't used to losing," Roush commented on his rookie's reality check. "There's a lot to learn when you come into this level of racing. It takes a lot of work and it takes some time. I'm not sure he realized all that when he came in."

Busch roared back onto a winning track in 2002, posting four checkered flags, a dozen top-fives, and 20 top-10s. He also finished third in series points. He won three of the season's last five races, including the finale at Homestead—where he would make NASCAR history two years later.

Despite four more wins, Busch cooled off in 2003, even though a fiery side of his personality ignited a couple of controversial incidents. He already had an image as an outsider, a Westerner who didn't fit the stereotypical "good ol' boy" role. He'd tangled in the past with Dale Earnhardt Jr. and Kevin Harvick, but then a long-running feud with veteran driver Jimmy Spencer flared up after an August event at Michigan International Speedway. Busch instigated some antics during the race, then the two confronted each other in the garage area afterward. After that incident, many fans viewed Busch as the villain, even though Spencer was the one who drew a suspension and was fined.

"It took me some time to understand the bigger picture," he admitted. "Racing at this level is one thing that I misunderstood the first couple of years."

By the time he hoisted the NASCAR NEXTEL Cup the next year in Florida, Busch had at least earned the respect, if not the love, of NASCAR fans. Earlier in the season they'd seen him withstand a blown motor in Atlanta, a spinout in Kansas, and a wreck in Charlotte. They had to appreciate his persistence. So how could anyone at Homestead not root for a guy who somehow overcame a disaster earlier in the race that nearly cost him the championship?

On lap 92 of the 267-lap battle for the championship, the front right tire on Busch's Ford broke clean off from the hub just as he was entering pit road. As the wheel rolled out onto the track, Busch came within inches of crashing into a pile of protective barrels. However, more good fortune was the yellow caution flag brought out by the stray tire, giving Busch a chance to pit and resume racing on the lead lap.

"We dodged a huge, devastating proposition that would have taken us out of this championship, and we pulled through," Busch said later, recognizing the hard work by his crew chief, Jimmy Fennig, and their pit team.

Although he restarted in 28th position, Busch wrangled his way back toward the front. Meanwhile, Johnson and Gordon needed to win the race to claim the championship. In the end, however, neither had enough, finishing second and third behind winner Biffle. Busch crossed the finish line fifth, giving him the NASCAR NEXTEL Cup Series title by a mere eight points—the closest margin of victory in 55 years of NASCAR.

"It's an unbelievable deal," an exhausted but overjoyed Busch said in Victory Lane. "This is what a team does to

## Kurt Busch
## Career Statistics

| Year | Starts | Wins | Top-5 Finishes | Total Points | Final Rank |
|------|--------|------|----------------|--------------|------------|
| 2000 | 7 | 0 | 0 | 513 | 48 |
| 2001 | 35 | 0 | 3 | 3,081 | 27 |
| 2002 | 36 | 4 | 12 | 4,641 | 3 |
| 2003 | 36 | 4 | 9 | 4,150 | 11 |
| 2004 | 36 | 3 | 10 | 6,506 | 1 |
| Total | 150 | 11 | 34 | | |

win a championship—they persevere on a day such as this. All year long we've done things like this, whether we put ourselves in a hole or whether we had a small problem. I just can't believe we were able to overcome all of that turmoil today."

Listening to so many cheers for him among the crowd of 70,000, Busch had to believe he'd finally won over a lot of new fans that memorable day, as well.

The newest NASCAR champion felt great all over.

# Here Comes Kyle!

Big brother Kurt Busch had better watch out, because little bro Kyle is zooming up behind him. While Kurt was stockpiling points in his quest for the 2004 NASCAR NEXTEL Cup Series championship, Kyle was setting rookie records in the series just below the NASCAR

NEXTEL Cup. At 19, he was the youngest full-time competitor in any of the top three divisions in NASCAR. Kyle came up just short of the title, finishing second to Martin Truex, Jr.

Nonetheless, Kyle's 5 wins, 16 top-five finishes, 22 top 10s, and 5 poles in the series just below the NASCAR NEXTEL Cup Series—along with Raybestos Rookie of the Year honors—convinced Hendrick Motorsports owner Rick Hendrick that the teenage

phenom was ready for the NASCAR NEXTEL Cup Series. In fact, Kyle ran six NASCAR NEXTEL Series races for Hendrick in 2004. Although he failed to finish four, he was chosen to replace veteran Terry Labonte in the No. 5 Chevrolet for the '05 season.

"The fact that I have this opportunity is amazing," said Kyle, who started racing when he was 13. He won two Legend Car track championships at Las Vegas Motor Speedway and, at 17, made his NASCAR debut in 2001, posting a pair of top-10 finishes in six starts. He credits Kurt with helping him learn the racing ropes, yet isn't adverse to some sibling rivalry now that they'll be competing against one another. "He goes out there and wins races, and I can do the same thing." Stay tuned.

# Chapter 6

# Elliott Sadler

Elliott Sadler's familiar No. 38 car is usually decorated with the bright green and red candies of his main sponsor, M&Ms candy. For Sadler in 2004, those two M's meant something else—more and more! In his sixth full season in the NASCAR NEXTEL Cup Series, after five consecutive finishes outside the top 20, Sadler zoomed ahead in 2004. Winning two races and finishing in the top five eight times, he made a huge move in his young career.

Sadler celebrated his 30th birthday on April 30 during the 2005 season, so he's got a lot of racing still ahead of him. In those 30 years, however, he also has a lot of racing behind him!

Elliott was born in Virginia. He started his racing career at the tender age of seven, driving go-karts. He moved up through other types of racing, racking up more than 200 victories before moving into stock cars

Elliott Sadler is one of the brightest stars in NASCAR.

in 1993. In 1995, he won his first season championship, capturing the Late Model Stock Car division at his home track in South Boston, Virginia.

Sadler was not just a great driver, but also a great athlete. A star basketball player in high school, he received a scholarship to attend James Madison University. However, Sadler suffered a severe knee injury that ended his basketball dreams. His racing dreams, however, kept zooming ahead.

With all that training behind him, it was time to move up to the big leagues. Debuting on the series just below the NASCAR NEXTEL Cup in 1997, he won three races and finished fifth overall. In 1998, he made his first start on the NASCAR NEXTEL Cup Series level. After his first full season in 1999, he came in second to Tony Stewart in the Raybestos Rookie of the Year voting. It looked as if the kid from Virginia was ready to roar right to the top of the NASCAR ranks, just as he had done back home.

But his first seasons in NASCAR were a struggle. He joined a team owned by the legendary Wood brothers, Glen and Len, but even their talents couldn't boost him into the top ranks. In 1999, 2000, and 2001, Sadler had only three top-10 finishes. One of those was his first victory, however, when he won the Food

A sweet finish for Elliott Sadler's No. 38 Ford!

City 500 at Bristol in Tennessee. Showing off some of the racing smarts gained on those small Virginia tracks (Bristol is only a half-mile long), he worked his way to the front from a 38th-place starting position. A late and quick pit stop helped propel him to his first win, the first by a Wood Brothers' racer since 1993.

However, that was a rare highlight. By the end of the 2002 season, it was clear that a change was in order if Sadler was to realize his racing dreams. He left the Wood Brothers team and joined Robert Yates Racing. It quickly proved to be a good match. He racked up two top-five finishes during the early part of the 2003 season. During that stretch Sadler achieved another first—capturing the pole position, which he did at Darlington Raceway.

Once again, however, disappointing results followed. He failed to finish in the top five again that season. A key moment in the season, and in his career, occurred in August, when Todd Parrott became Sadler's new crew chief. Parrott was a veteran of many years on pit road, and his expertise, combined with Sadler's driving ability, would prove to be a winning combination.

Their first season together, 2004, got off to a fast start, as Sadler qualified on the front row at the

Daytona and eventually finished seventh. But through the next two months, it seemed as if Sadler were driving a roller coaster instead of a stock car.

"I came here to try to win a championship," he said of switching to Yates. "And it was just up and down all year long. A lot of times I looked at myself in the mirror and wondered, 'Have I made the right decision?'"

He would do well one week, then poorly the next, a pattern he repeated all season long. For instance, he followed a 14th-place finish at Bristol with his second career victory in the Samsung/Radio Shack 400 in Texas. Of the next four races, he never finished above 12th. The good part of this pattern was that his high finishes were keeping him in the chase. He was never lower than 10th place in the season standings.

However, his erratic finishes made him and his team worry that they would not hold a top-10 spot long enough to qualify for the 2004 Chase for the NASCAR NEXTEL Cup.

Then came the most important race of the season for Sadler—the Pop Secret 400 at California Speedway in Fontana. A third-place finish three weeks earlier in the Brickyard 400 had been the only highlight for him and his team for 10 weeks. It was time to make a big move to secure a spot in the final 10 contenders for the championship. And Sadler came through, using what he called "the best move I've probably ever made as a race car driver." With new tires after a pit stop, he roared up on the outside to pass Brian Vickers and Mark Martin with only a few laps to go. He held on for his third career victory, which clinched his place in the Chase for the NASCAR NEXTEL Cup.

In those final 10 races, Sadler's results mirrored the rest of his season. Unfortunately, his roller-coaster ride ended near the bottom, not the top. After starting

out in sixth position in the top 10, he rose as high as fourth, before a series of mishaps ended his chances. A crash at Martinsville left him unable to finish the race. A pit road accident the next week damaged his car and placed him farther back in the pack. And he ran into the wall at Phoenix to essentially end his championship chances.

But Sadler learned a lot during the Chase, lessons that will serve the young driver well as he continues to rise in the NASCAR ranks.

"It's been great racing," he said of his Chase for the NASCAR NEXTEL Cup experience. "It's been fun. It's been hectic. It's been nerve-wracking. I was about to throw up before every race!"

While he continues to gain notice for his fine driving, Sadler also got some attention off the track when he let his normally short-cropped hair grow and grow. By the time the season ended, everyone in the pits was calling him "Shaggy."

"I decided to just let it grow and then bleach it like [country music star] Keith Urban. I'll do that mostly during the hunting season, when no one will see me, and we'll see what it ends up looking like," he said in 2004 with a laugh. It's a sure bet that his brother, Hermie, also a NASCAR NEXTEL Cup driver with 40 starts under his belt through 2004, will be there in the pits to tease him about it.

Sadler is a hunting fan and spends most of his off-season in the woods with his Walker hunting dogs, which he raises. Whether he has long hair or short hair under his helmet or his hunting cap, Sadler also takes more than 20 years of racing experience out to the track. For a man who is still a pretty young driver, that's a huge advantage. As he continues to move up in the NASCAR NEXTEL Cup Series ranks, look for Sadler to win M&M, as in more and more races!

# Elliott Sadler
## Career Statistics

| Year | Starts | Wins | Top-5 Finishes | Total Points | Final Rank |
|------|--------|------|------|------|------|
| 1998 | 2 | 0 | 0 | | |
| 1999 | 34 | 0 | 0 | 3,191 | 24 |
| 2000 | 33 | 0 | 0 | 2,762 | 29 |
| 2001 | 36 | 1 | 3 | 3,471 | 20 |
| 2002 | 36 | 0 | 2 | 3,418 | 23 |
| 2003 | 36 | 0 | 2 | 3,525 | 22 |
| 2004 | 36 | 2 | 8 | 6,024 | 9 |
| Total | 213 | 3 | 15 | | |

# "Happy" to Be Here

Like Elliott Sadler, Kevin Harvick is a young driver who has gone through his share of ups and downs. However, he still has plenty of skills that could take him to the top. Kevin made his NASCAR NEXTEL Cup Series debut in 2001 driving for the powerful Richard Childress team. He was taking the place of the legendary Dale Earnhardt Sr. Kevin filled those shoes pretty well for a kid, winning two races, including one at Atlanta in just his third start in the NASCAR

NEXTEL Cup Series. He finished ninth overall and was named the Raybestos Rookie of the Year. Big things were expected from the guy nicknamed "Happy."

But his second season was not as strong. He added a victory in Chicago, but fell to 21st overall.

In 2003, he bounced back, winning the Brickyard 400 and notching a career-best 11 top-five finishes to wind up fifth overall. Things were looking up for Kevin.

However, in 2004, the roller coaster went down again. Kevin suffered through a long and difficult season, going without a win for the first time in his short career and finishing in the top five only five times. Harvick missed out on taking part in the Chase for the NASCAR NEXTEL Cup, something he'll try to avoid in coming years.

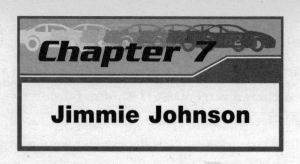

# Chapter 7

## Jimmie Johnson

Jimmie Johnson has been going fast his whole life. After trying a variety of other types of racing, he finally found his home in stock cars. And he's kept going fast in NASCAR, too. After starting with a first full-time season (2001) that was one of the best ever, he has become one of the top drivers in NASCAR NEXTEL Cup Series racing. Here's the story of this quick-moving young driver. Pay attention…it goes by pretty fast!

Johnson, unlike most top drivers, was born not in the Southeast, but in southern California. He began racing mini-bikes on dirt tracks when he was just four years old! He drove bigger and faster motorcycles as he grew older, often taking on tough desert and off-road courses.

He moved up to trucks in his late teens, driving in desert races as well as stadium off-road courses.

Look for Jimmie Johnson to be a challenger for a
NASCAR NEXTEL Cup Series championship.

In 1997, he switched to American Speed Association races, which are smaller stock cars that race on smaller asphalt or dirt tracks. In 1998, he was the Raybestos Rookie of the Year in that series. His success there caught the eye of a driver whose name is familiar to all NASCAR fans—Jeff Gordon.

"Jeff approached me about driving one of the Hendrick team cars," Johnson said. It was a dream come true for Johnson, who had grown up watching Gordon win several championships.

"Growing up in California, racing in the desert, I would watch Jeff win his championships and wonder 'How in the world do I get there?'" With Jeff's help, he would make his stock car dreams come true. However, he had still many more miles ahead of him on that road.

In 1999, he finished third in the ASA standings. At the same time, he began racing in the series just below the NASCAR NEXTEL Cup Series. He finished 10th in that series in 1999 and earned his first race win in 2000 at Chicagoland Speedway.

The 2002 season was an important one for Johnson. His teammate, Gordon, and car owner, Rick Hendrick, felt that the former desert racer was ready for the big time—the NASCAR NEXTEL Cup Series.

Now Johnson would not only be racing in the top series in NASCAR, he would be a teammate and employee of his hero, Jeff Gordon.

"At first it was intimidating," Johnson said. "I went from watching Jeff race on TV to having him as a boss. [Gordon was co-owner of Johnson's No. 48 car.] He was a tremendous help to me, though, teaching me about life on and off the track. I'd be foolish if I didn't use a resource like him."

Johnson learned his lessons well. In February 2002, he became the first rookie in race history to win the pole position at the fabled Daytona 500. "Winning the pole there was one of the highlights of my career," he said after finishing 15th in the race. "I hope one of these days I'll get my car into Victory Lane there, too."

Johnson did make it to Victory Lane two months later by winning the NAPA Auto Parts 500. In front of family and friends at the California Speedway, not far from his hometown, he roared under the checkered flag for his first NASCAR NEXTEL Cup Series victory.

After the race, Johnson's teammate, boss, and friend, Jeff Gordon, said, "I knew Jimmie had a lot of talent, but I never knew the team and Jimmie would come together so quickly."

Later, Johnson told lowesracing.com, "Winning

Jimmie Johnson's No. 48 race car crossing the finish line ahead of the pack has become a familiar sight.

was awesome! The funny thing is, I thought when I won my first race, I would feel some sort of satisfaction, like I had accomplished something huge. However, the following day, I just felt hungrier for more wins. Winning makes you want to win more."

Even as he kept looking for ways to feed that hunger, Johnson also knew that he still had a lot to learn. In an interview on NASCAR.com that summer, he spoke about the jump he had made into the "big leagues" of stock car racing. "There are a lot of things outside the car that change. Inside the car, that's the part you look forward to and have grown up dreaming about. Outside the car, you have no clue what's coming. There are responsibilities to your sponsor [Lowe's Home Improvement Stores], your team, your fans, and the media. I find myself extremely busy. I have to make sure to learn to focus my mind on the race just before it starts."

While he learned lessons about life off the track, he was still learning on the track, too. He made some mistakes, such as missing his pit area or spinning out, that cost him races. However, he just kept going fast, as he had always done. At the MBNA Platinum 400 in Delaware he won his second race of the season, zooming to second place in the season points standings.

In September, the series returned to Delaware for another race and Johnson returned to Victory Lane, winning the MBNA All-American Heroes 400. He became the first rookie to win both races there in one season, and the second driver ever to win three races in his rookie season. Johnson credited his crew for this latest victory. "It all came down to our last pit stop," he said afterward. "They got us out first and I was able to hang on."

With a 10th-place finish at Kansas in late September, Johnson became the first rookie in NASCAR history to lead in the points standings. He only lasted in the top spot for a week, finishing no better than sixth in the season's final six races. Finishing fifth overall, he also lost out in the Raybestos Rookie of the Year race, as Ryan Newman slipped ahead of him in points. Johnson's experience in 2002, both good and bad, taught him many lessons, lessons that he quickly put to work.

In 2003, Johnson won two more races, both of them at New Hampshire International Speedway. He was also in the top five 14 times, more than one-third of his starts. The lessons he had learned as a rookie were making him a more consistent, steady driver. He was the only driver in the series to spend the entire season in the top 10. With a string of six straight top-three finishes to end the year, he wound up in second place, 90 points behind champion Matt Kenseth. Second place in only his second season? It was a pretty impressive record. What was even more impressive was that he finished two spots ahead of a certain No. 24 driver who he shared garage space. That's right—student-employee Johnson outpointed teacher-boss Jeff Gordon. Johnson also raked in more than $7.7 million in prize money!

For 2004, NASCAR instituted the Chase for the NASCAR NEXTEL Cup. It was tailor-made for Johnson. The new plan meant that after 26 races, only the top 10 drivers at that point would be competing in the final 10 races for the NASCAR NEXTEL Cup title. Including the 2004 season, Johnson was ranked in the top 10 for all but two weeks since first reaching that level in the fifth race of his rookie year. That meant he was in the top 10 for 103 of 105 weeks! Once he jumped back into the top 10 in that fifth week, he never left it.

Johnson had his best season ever in 2004, winning eight races, finishing in the top 10 23 times. He entered the Chase for the NASCAR NEXTEL Cup in second place overall behind—who else?—Jeff Gordon.

But after four races in the Chase for the NASCAR NEXTEL Cup competition, Johnson was struggling in eighth place. It looked like his dream season would end in a nightmare. Then, like an off-road truck charging through the desert, Jimmie put the pedal to the metal. He won three races in a row and four of the next five. When Johnson notched his final win of that streak in the Mountain Dew Southern 500 in the next-to-last race of the year, he had a real shot at the title.

He entered the Ford 400 in Miami trailing points leader Kurt Busch by just 18 points. A victory in sunny Florida would give Johnson his longed-for championship. He ran a great race, finishing second behind Greg Biffle. It was not enough. For the second year in a row, Johnson finished the season in second place, only eight points behind Busch. That made it the closest finish in NASCAR history.

So, in his first three seasons in the NASCAR NEXTEL Cup Series, Johnson finished fifth, second, and second. Not bad for an former desert rat!

## Jimmie Johnson Career Statistics

| Year | Starts | Wins | Top-5 Finishes | Total Points | Final Rank |
|------|--------|------|----------------|--------------|------------|
| 2001 | 3 | 0 | 0 | 210 | 52 |
| 2002 | 36 | 3 | 6 | 4,600 | 5 |
| 2003 | 36 | 3 | 14 | 4,932 | 2 |
| 2004 | 36 | 8 | 20 | 6,498 | 2 |
| Total | 111 | 14 | 40 | | |

# Dueling in the Dirt

When most people look at a desert, they see sand, cactus, a few bare trees, acres and acres of rocks, dirt, and, well, pretty much nothing else. When Jimmie Johnson looks at a desert, he sees a racetrack.

The California native got his first taste of racing success in those early desert races. He bounced along in pickup trucks, dune buggies, and other vehicles on demanding off-road courses. These rugged racetracks are a far cry from the smooth surfaces of NASCAR tracks. The goal, however, is still the same: go faster than the other guy and get to the finish line first.

Johnson raced in extreme heat, dusty wind, and featureless landscapes and loved every minute of it.

"I've always enjoyed racing off-road trucks in the desert. It's where I first learned to race. There is something about the challenge of trying to control a race car at high speeds while going over extremely rough terrain." All the while, though, he had one eye on the finish line and one eye on the future.

"I was out there in the Nevada desert and it was 120 degrees and I was beating around in an off-road truck wondering what it would take to get to the next

level," he told the Los Angeles Times in 2004. In 2002, with Jeff Gordon's help, he got his chance and he left the desert in his rear-view mirror.

# Chapter 8

## Kasey Kahne

His sparkling blue eyes and baby face are a mask. Behind that mask, however, Kasey Kahne's pop-idol looks disguise a tough-as-nails young driver, ready to take on anyone at any time. The 2004 Raybestos Rookie of the Year is surely a name to watch as NASCAR races into future seasons.

Kasey got his start in racing in his home state of Washington. When he was 14, he won four races in only his first season of racing! At the time, he was driving cars called micro midgets, which are smaller than regular cars, but capable of speeds of up to 60 miles per hour. Two years later, he moved up to mini-sprint and sprint cars. These open-wheel cars race on quarter-mile tracks, with tight turns and cars constantly jostling for position. Kasey quickly succeeded there, too, winning an impressive 11 out of 14 races in 1996.

Kasey Kahne was the NASCAR Raybestos Rookie of the Year in 2004.

He kept moving up the racing ladder. His next stop was a sprint car circuit in which he won 12 races, almost all against drivers older than he was. In 2000, he won his first national championship, capturing the United States Auto Club midget car championship by winning nine races. In 2001, he spent time behind the wheel in three different series, adding more and more wins.

Kasey's made his debut in the series just below the NASCAR NEXTEL Cup in 2002. Kasey found the going a bit tougher than in his earlier race career, and he struggled as a rookie. He cracked the top 10 in only one race in 2002, finishing 33rd in the season standings. However, the same drive and skills that had made him a champion by the age of 16 continued to serve him well in NASCAR. In 2003, he took his first checkered flag in a NASCAR race, winning the Ford 300 at Homestead-Miami Speedway. He roared into the top five four times and notched 14 top-10 finishes. At the end of the year, he was in seventh place overall. Kasey had one more stop on his ladder of success: the NASCAR NEXTEL Cup Series.

For 2004, he joined the legendary Ray Evernham's Dodge team. Evernham had been the crew chief for Jeff Gordon during several of his championship seasons, and has the reputation of being one of the top engine-builders around. Kasey was taking the place—and the No. 9 car—of Bill Elliott, a popular veteran driver. It was a perfect situation for a young driver like Kasey—having an experienced team leader and a veteran driver who could help show him the ropes.

"I couldn't think of a better way to grow as a driver than working with a leader as great as Ray Evernham," Kasey said.

During the season, Kasey kept a diary on his web site (kaseykahne.com). After his first race, the legendary Daytona 500, he recorded his thoughts.

"As the drivers were introduced, I was behind Ricky Craven. I took a glance to see what he did on stage. I wanted to make sure I knew the routine. No rookie mistakes! I stepped out on stage. I could hear the applause and cheers. It might not have been as loud as the other drivers . . . but to this rookie, it sure sounded loud!"

Kasey took full advantage of the great car and the special insights from Elliott to roar into his rookie season. In just his second NASCAR NEXTEL Cup Series race, the Subway 400 at North Carolina Speedway, Kasey finished second. A week later in Las Vegas, he captured the pole position at the UAW-DaimlerChrysler 400 with a track qualifying record. He finished second again. He followed that with a third-place finish at the Golden Corral 400 at Atlanta. His trio of top-five finishes in his first four starts had not been accomplished in more than 40 years!

After only four weeks in the world's top stock car series, the 23-year-old found himself fourth overall in the standings! He had come a long way in a short time.

However, Kasey found that the NASCAR NEXTEL Cup Series season was itself a long one. He added two more second-place finishes before the halfway point, but those were the only highlights, as he struggled in many other races.

Starting with the Siemens 300 at New Hampshire, however, he racked up top-10 finishes in six of the next nine races. After the Pop Secret 400 in California, Kasey suddenly found himself in ninth place. With one more qualifying race to go, the rookie had a shot at joining the "big boys" for the inaugural Chase for the

**Kasey Kahne drives the No. 9 Dodge—real fast!**

NASCAR NEXTEL Cup. However, at the Chevy Rock and Roll 400 at Richmond, Kasey finished 24th. That result dropped him to 12th overall, knocking him out of the Chase.

Close-but-not-close-enough was the theme of his 2004 season. Kasey racked up five impressive, but ultimately frustrating, second-place finishes. Before the final race in Miami, he reflected on his first season and the number of near-misses.

"Everybody talks about luck and this and that," Kahne said. "I don't know if it's luck or it's just not our time yet or whatever it is. Sooner or later we'll win. I don't know when that will be, but I don't think we're missing much. I think we have a great race team. A lot of times when we didn't win it wasn't because of a bad pit stop or something out on the track. It's part of the ups and downs [of racing]. We've had a lot of ups and downs this year. We're ready to win."

Kahne didn't win or make the Chase, and the young driver and his team were disappointed, but they didn't stop giving 100% in the remaining races in the season. Though they couldn't capture the championship, there was still one big award to shoot for—the Raybestos Rookie of the Year selection. With every race meaning much more during the Chase,

## Kasey Kahne Career Statistics

| Year | Starts | Wins | Top-5 Finishes | Total Points | Final Rank |
|------|--------|------|----------------|--------------|------------|
| 2004 | 36 | 0 | 14 | 4,264 | 13th |
| Total | 36 | 0 | 14 | | |

Kasey found himself among the leaders often. (Kasey also took time out for some other racing. The week before the final NASCAR NEXTEL Cup race at Miami, he won his first and second races in the NASCAR Craftsman Truck Series, capturing the Darlington 200 and Ford 200.) Back in NASCAR NEXTEL Cup Series, he finished fifth in three of the season's final four races. His final total of 4,264 points was good enough for 13th place and he was named the Raybestos Rookie of the Year.

In his Web diary, Kasey summed up his season. "I've enjoyed this season a lot. I definitely have higher expectations for next year [2005] and I think our whole team will. I expect to run in the top 10 more consistently and have more opportunities to win races. I want to be in the top 10 at the end of the year and have the opportunity to run for the championship."

Over the course of the year, Kasey had been very busy. He started all 36 NASCAR NEXTEL Cup races, plus 34 in the series just below the NASCAR NEXTEL Cup. Toss in two truck races, and he competed in 72 races in about 40 weeks! After a much-deserved winter vacation, Kasey looked forward to the 2005 season, which he hoped would bring him his first trip to Victory Lane in a NASCAR NEXTEL Cup Series race. He has won in every other kind of vehicle he has driven, so there's every reason to expect that he'll do that very soon.

# New Faces in the NASCAR NEXTEL Cup Series

Every year, new drivers appear in NASCAR races, and they all share the same ambition—to win. The 2005 season is no exception, as a group of up-and-coming drivers take aim at the checkered flag. Keep an eye out for these future stars.

Along with Kyle Busch (see page 74), these up and coming drivers are set to make their mark on NASCAR NEXTEL Cup Series racing.

**Carl Edwards:** Carl quickly made his presence felt in NASCAR NEXTEL Cup Series racing. In only his fifth race at the top level, he roared around Jimmie Johnson to capture the checkered flag at the Golden Corral 500 at Atlanta in March 2005. In Atlanta, Edwards' teammates cheered him on when he climbed out of his No. 99 car. He stood on the window opening, balanced himself, and—flip!—stuck the landing like an Olympic gymnast! And there's no doubt—NASCAR fans have certainly flipped for Edwards, too.

**Jason Leffler**: Car owner Joe Gibbs knows how to pick winners. He already has former champs Bobby Labonte and Tony Stewart on this team. For 2005, he

signed young Jason Leffler to join that duo. Jason has had success in cars and trucks in other NASCAR series.

**Scott Riggs**: Here's a NASCAR success story: A young driver excels on Wisconsin short tracks. He moves up to the series just below the NASCAR NEXTEL Cup. He is noticed by team owners and gets a shot at the big time. Sound familiar? That's the story of Matt Kenseth, but it's also the story of Scott Riggs. Scott drove the No. 22 car to a top-30 finish in his first full season of NASCAR NEXTEL Cup Series racing in 2004. Now he'll be aiming to join Matt atop the winner's stand at the end of the season.

**Brian Vickers**: Only Kasey Kahne outpointed Brian Vickers among 2004 NASCAR NEXTEL Cup Series rookies. The year before, when Brian was just 19, he became the youngest NASCAR champion ever, when he won the championship in the series just below

Carl Edwards

the NASCAR NEXTEL Cup. His skill at posting high qualifying times—he earned two pole positions in 2004—gives him a leg up on other young drivers.

Scott Riggs

# PHOTOGRAPHY CREDITS

All photographs including cover images by **Sherryl Creekmore/NASCAR** except for the following. Pages 21, 51, and 52 by **CIA Stock Photography, Inc.**, and page 110 by **Streeter Lecka/Getty Images for NASCAR**.